JOHN F. KENNEDY
The Making of a LEADER

By the Editors of TIME For Kids
WITH RITU UPADHYAY

HarperCollins*Publishers*

About the Author: Before moving to Delhi, India, where she is a freelance journalist, Ritu Upadhyay was an editor with TIME FOR KIDS. Born and raised in Chicago, she has always been fascinated with the Kennedys and the legacy the family has created.

John F. Kennedy
Copyright © 2005 by Time Inc.
Used under exclusive license by HarperCollins Publishers Inc.
Manufactured in China by South China Printing Company Ltd.

LIBRARY OF CONGRESS CATALOGING-IN-PUBLICATION DATA

John F. Kennedy : the making of a leader / by the editors of Time for Kids with Ritu Upadhyay.— 1st ed.
p. cm.
ISBN 0-06-057602-2 (pbk.) — ISBN 0-06-057603-0 (trade) 1. Kennedy, John F. (John Fitzgerald), 1917–1963—Juvenile literature. 2. Presidents—United States—Biography—Juvenile literature. [1. Kennedy, John F. (John Fitzgerald), 1917–1963.
2. Presidents.] I. Upadhyay, Ritu. II. Time for kids online.
E842.Z9J68 2005
973.922'092—dc22   2003026552

7 8 9 10
First Edition

Photography and Illustration Credits:
Cover: JFK Collection—Zuma—Newscom; cover inset: Bettmann—Corbis; cover flap: AP Photo; title page: Time Life Pictures—Getty Images; contents page: Time Life Pictures—Getty Images; p. iv: AP Photo—John F. Kennedy National Historic Site; p.1: Library of Congress; p.2: Corbis; (photo corners): Photodisc; p.3: The John F. Kennedy Library; p.4: Corbis; p.5: The John F. Kennedy Library; p.6 (bottom left): Photodisc; p.6–7: The John F. Kennedy Library; p.7: Corbis; p.8: The John F. Kennedy Library; p.8 (bottom right): public domain; p.9: Culver Pictures; p.10 (top): The John F. Kennedy Library; p.10 (bottom left): Photodisc; p.11: The John F. Kennedy Library; p.12: The John F. Kennedy Library; p.13 (top): AP Photo; p.13 (bottom right): The John F. Kennedy Library; p.14: The John F. Kennedy Library; p.15: The John F. Kennedy Library; p.16: The John F. Kennedy Library; p.17 (bottom): public domain; p.17 (Fast Facts, top-bottom): Archive Photos—Newscom, Library of Congress, Chris Kleponis—Newscom, Time Life Pictures, Bettmann—Corbis; p.18: The John F. Kennedy Library; p.19: The John F. Kennedy Library; p.20: The John F. Kennedy Library; p.21: Hulton Archive—Getty Images; p.22: The John F. Kennedy Library; p.23: The John F. Kennedy Library; p.24: The John F. Kennedy Library; p.25 (bottom left): The John F. Kennedy Library; p.25 (inset): Bettmann—Corbis; p.26: Bettmann—Corbis; p.27: Bettmann—Corbis; p.28 (top): Smithsonian National Air and Space Museum; p.28 (bottom TV Frame): Photodisc; (photo): Time Life Pictures—Getty Images; p.29: The John F. Kennedy Library; p.30: Time Life Pictures—Getty Images; p.31 (top): The John F. Kennedy Library; p.31 (bottom left): Flip Schulke—Corbis; p.32: Time Life Pictures—Getty Images; p.33: Time Life Pictures—Getty Images; p.34: The John F. Kennedy Library; p.35: Hulton Archive—Getty Images; p.36: The John F. Kennedy Library; p.37 (top): Bettmann—Corbis; p.37 (bottom left): The John F. Kennedy Library; p.38 (top): Wally McNamee—Corbis; p.38 (bottom left): Bettmann—Corbis; p.39: AP Photo; p.40: JFK Collection—Zuma—Newscom; p.41 (top): Life Magazine—Time Inc.; p.41 (bottom right): Image Library; p.41 (bottom left): public domain; p.42: courtesy of Hugh Sidey; p.43 (top): AFP—Newscom; p.43 (bottom): Black Star; p.44 (top to bottom): Library of Congress; Corbis; AP Photo; Photoplay Archives/LGI; back cover: Library of Congress

Acknowledgments:
For TIME FOR KIDS: Editorial Director: Keith Garton; Editor: Jonathan Rosenbloom; Art Director: Rachel Smith; Photography Editor: Sandy Perez

 Find out more at www.timeforkids.com/bio/kennedy

CONTENTS

CHAPTER 1　**The Early Years** 1

CHAPTER 2　**The Making of a Leader** 6

CHAPTER 3　**Entering Politics** 12

CHAPTER 4　**The Race for President** 16

CHAPTER 5　**Life at the White House** 20

CHAPTER 6　**Trouble Around the World** 26

CHAPTER 7　**The Country Moves Ahead** 30

CHAPTER 8　**A Tragic Trip** 36

INTERVIEW　**Talking About Kennedy** 42

TIME LINE　**John F. Kennedy's Key Dates** 44

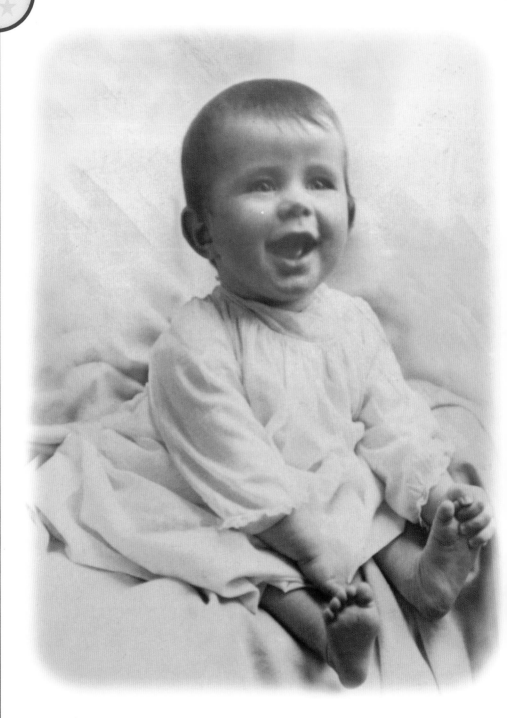

▲ JOHN F. KENNEDY was only a few months old when this photograph was taken. He was the second child of Joseph and Rose Kennedy.

The Early
YEARS

O n a cold spring day in Brookline, Massachusetts, a baby was born in the big frame house at 83 Beals Street. It was just a little after 3 P.M. on May 29, 1917, when John Fitzgerald Kennedy came into the world.

Jack, as his parents nicknamed him, was the second child of Joseph and Rose Kennedy. The baby was born into a rich and well-known family. His father was a successful businessman. His mother was the daughter of the mayor of Boston.

> **"***Ask not what your country can do for you, but rather what you can do for your country.***"**
>
> JOHN F. KENNEDY

From the very beginning, little Jack was thin and sickly. When he was three, he almost died of an illness called scarlet fever. For a month his parents prayed by his bedside. He got better, but for the rest of his life he was always suffering from one sickness or another. His family used to tease him and say that if a mosquito were to bite Jack, the mosquito would die.

A Growing Family

Over the years, the Kennedy family grew to include nine children—four boys and five girls. The brood moved to a house with twelve rooms. Rose had to be very strict with her children so things wouldn't get out of control. Meals were served only at set times. If any children arrived late, they would not be able to have the food that had already been served. Rose also wanted the children to look neat and clean. Young freckle-faced Jack didn't like this. His thick hair tumbled messily across his forehead. He hardly ever tucked in his shirt. His friend Lem Billings remembered that, as a kid, Jack was "usually tardy, forgetful, and often . . . sloppy."

Since Jack had so many brothers and sisters, his childhood was full of fun and activity. The Kennedys

▲ BABY JACK sits on a Massachusetts beach in 1918. The sea was always an important part of his life.

▲ **THE KENNEDYS SPENT SUMMERS** in Hyannis Port, where they swam and sailed. They also played against one another in sports such as touch football and tennis. Jack is the boy in the white shirt on the left.

spent their summers at a home in Hyannis Port, Massachusetts, a small town by the ocean. They learned to love the sea. Joseph wanted his children to do well at everything. "We want winners around here," he would say. That was a lesson the children would remember as they grew up.

There was a lot of friendly competition in the family. Jack used to get in many fistfights with Joe Jr., his older brother. Joe Jr. was bigger and stronger and could beat up Jack, who was small for his age. Outside the family, though, the Kennedy children were very loyal to one

another. Joe Jr. became Jack's coach and protector.

Jack didn't like being bossed around all the time, but secretly he admired his big brother.

At dinner the family would talk about politics and current events. Joe Jr. took part in mealtime debates with their father. From an early age he stood out as the young star in the family. He even said that one day he would become President. Jack, on the other hand, would rather play tricks than talk politics.

Good Old-Fashioned Values

Both parents often reminded the kids that the United States had been good to the Kennedys. Two of Jack's great-grandfathers sailed from Ireland to the United States in the 1800s to seek a better life. Rose said, "Whatever good things the family received from the country, you should return by performing some service for the country."

Even though Jack's father was very rich, he refused to spoil his children with large allowances. He wanted them to learn the value of money. When Jack was about eleven, he decided he needed more money. He wrote his father a letter titled, "A Plea for a Raise, by Jack Kennedy." He carefully explained how he was spending the forty cents a week he already earned. But, he said, as a Boy Scout, he needed more money to buy supplies. "I have to buy canteens, blankets, searchlights—things that will last me for years," he wrote. Jack's father agreed to the raise after reading his son's convincing letter. Jack proved he could write well and could persuade people with his words. That would serve him well for the rest of his life.

▶ COPS AND ROBBERS
Jack used to dress up as a police officer. He was always getting into mischief and playing good-natured tricks on people.

The Making of a
LEADER

When Jack was ten, he was sent away to Choate, a private school in Connecticut. He lived there and came home for holidays. Jack had developed a love of reading during all those days spent sick in bed as a young child. But in school he got only average grades. He was always thought of as the little brother of Joe Jr., who made better grades and was better at sports. Jack often was in trouble for not listening to his teachers. But he was gifted at making friends. It was hard to resist his cheerful personality. One of his

▶ FOOTBALL was an important family sport. Jack is about ten years old in this picture. The "D" stands for Dexter School, where he went before Choate.

former teachers remembered, "When he flashed his smile, he could charm a bird off a tree."

After Choate he decided to go to Harvard University in Cambridge, Massachusetts, like his father and brother. Jack was popular at the school, but he still didn't get very good grades.

In 1938, during Jack's third year of college, President Franklin D. Roosevelt named Joseph Kennedy Sr. the American ambassador to Great Britain. (An ambassador is a representative in a foreign country.) Jack went to England to visit his father. He traveled to many countries in Europe. He met lots of people and

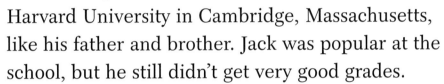

7

listened to their opinions about current events. When he returned to Harvard, he wrote a paper about why England did not stand up to the German dictator, Adolph Hitler. His paper became a best-selling book, *Why England Slept*, in 1940.

Jack wasn't sure what to do after he graduated from Harvard. He had studied American government, but he didn't want to go to law school. He decided to join the U.S. Navy in 1941. Three months later, the Japanese bombed Pearl Harbor, Hawaii—the headquarters of the Pacific fleet. When that happened, the United States entered World War II. Jack rose to the rank of commander in the navy.

WHY
ENGLAND
SLEPT

JOHN F. KENNEDY

▲ ON DECEMBER 7, 1941, Japanese planes bombed Pearl Harbor, Hawaii, in a surprise attack. The next day the United States entered World War II.

Jack Becomes a Hero

On August 2, 1943, Jack faced the biggest challenge of his life. The patrol boat Jack was in charge of got separated from the other American forces in the Pacific Ocean. At 2:30 A.M. a Japanese ship suddenly plowed through the small boat and cut it in half. Two of Jack's crew died. Three were badly hurt. The survivors floated in the water, holding on to a piece of the boat all night. Jack decided their only chance to live was to swim to a nearby small island. One man was too injured and weak to move. Jack clenched the straps of

▲ SETTING SAIL on
PT 109, the small ship
Jack commanded

the man's lifejacket between his teeth and towed him to safety. He swam like that for five hours, until they reached the shore of the island. Days later the crew was rescued. Jack returned to the United States and was given two important medals for his courage and leadership. One was the Navy and Marine Corps Medal. The other was the Purple Heart Medal. The Kennedys were proud of their son and brother, and they were very grateful that he returned from the war alive.

Dad's Big Dream

In the spring of 1944, the Kennedy family received terrible news. Joe Jr., who was serving in the air force, was killed while flying on a dangerous mission. Joe Sr. was very upset by the death. He had had big dreams for his eldest son. As time passed, Joe Sr. convinced Jack that now it was his duty to go into politics. His father told him he wanted Jack to be the country's first Roman Catholic President. Some people thought a Roman Catholic could never be elected President of the United States. Years later these people would be proved wrong.

▶ **ANCHORS AWEIGH!**
Jack Kennedy poses proudly in his navy uniform. He served as a commander.

11

Entering
POLITICS

Jack rose to his father's challenge. In 1946 he ran for the United States House of Representatives from his home state of Massachusetts. The entire family helped with the campaign. His father asked his

powerful and wealthy friends for support. Jack's mother gave tea parties for women in the community. Jack and his

◀ RUNNING FOR CONGRESS was John Kennedy's first try at public office. The issues that were important to him are written on the banner behind him. He won!

▲ JACK liked nothing better than going out and meeting people in their hometowns. It gave him a good idea of what issues were important to them.

brothers and sisters knocked on doors asking for people's votes. The hard work, and the famous Kennedy name, paid off. Jack won the election in November.

In Washington twenty-nine-year-old Congressman Kennedy stood out as a young, handsome politician. But as always, he was in bad health. Doctors decided he had

▶ BACK PAIN didn't stop Kennedy from giving speeches while running for office.

Addison's disease, an illness that destroys part of the adrenal glands. Addison's disease made Kennedy too weak to fight off other sicknesses. The Kennedy family kept the disease a secret. They feared it would put an end to Jack's political career. Kennedy also had serious back pain but was able to deal with it by taking many kinds of medicine.

Jack and Jackie Get Married

In 1952 Kennedy ran for the United States Senate and won. At the same time he was dating a beautiful young newspaper photographer. Her name was Jacqueline Bouvier. Like Kennedy she came from a wealthy family. She was intelligent, graceful, and stylish. The handsome senator asked Jackie to be his wife. Their marriage on September 12, 1953, was one of the most talked about events of the year.

In 1954 Kennedy had to have a serious back operation. During the months he spent in the hospital recovering, he wrote a book, *Profiles in Courage*. It described

▲ **SIGN HERE!**
People often asked Kennedy to autograph his book.

▲ JACK AND JACKIE's wedding reception took place at Jackie's family home in Rhode Island. The wedding was reported in many magazines and newspapers.

the bravery of a few politicians who fought for their ideals to make the United States a better place in which to live. Kennedy later won the Pulitzer Prize in biography, one of the nation's top writing prizes. The senator proved he was a charming politician *and* an intelligent writer.

The Race For

PRESIDENT

After getting experience in Congress, Kennedy, with the urging of his family, decided it was time to run for President. In July 1960 he won the Democratic Party's nomination for the race. With the help of his younger brother Robert, Kennedy ran a strong campaign. He promised a "new frontier" for Americans. Kennedy and his running mate, Lyndon Baines Johnson of Texas, ran

▲ CAMPAIGNING in New Hampshire, Kennedy tried to get people to vote for him.

against Richard Nixon, the Republican Party's choice. Nixon was much older and more experienced than Kennedy. He was serving as the Vice President of the United States under Dwight D. Eisenhower. But Kennedy used his youth to his advantage. The first ever presidential debates on television were held during the 1960 election. On television Kennedy looked handsome and smart. He spoke well and

▲ PEOPLE who wanted Kennedy to win the election wore this button.

The Constitution states that no one can be President of the United States unless he or she is at least thirty-five years old. Here are the five youngest presidents. (Note: Vice President Theodore Roosevelt became President when William McKinley died in office.)

Theodore Roosevelt
42

John F. Kennedy
43

Bill Clinton
46

Ulysses S. Grant
46

Grover Cleveland
47

had a lot of energy. Richard Nixon came off as tired, old, and unprepared.

It was a very close race, but Kennedy won. At the age of forty-three, John Fitzgerald Kennedy became the thirty-fifth President of the United States. He was the youngest man ever elected to the highest office in the land.

THE 35TH
U.S. PRESIDENT

Kennedy came to Washington, D.C., with new and exciting ideas. One of his greatest ideas was starting the Peace Corps. He urged Americans to volunteer to work in countries around the world. The volunteers served as teachers to help people in poorer nations improve their lives. Peace Corps workers taught people to read and write. They taught better ways to farm, and how to lead healthier lives.

More than forty years after the Peace Corps began, volunteers today are still helping others who are less fortunate.

Kennedy was sworn in as President of the United States on January 20, 1961. It was a very cold day, and eight inches of snow covered the capital! But Kennedy managed to warm the hearts of most of the people who watched him. His famous inauguration speech was one of the most memorable of all time. Kennedy challenged Americans to "ask not what your country can do for you, but rather what you can do for your country." His speech inspired Americans to be active citizens and to make the United States and the world a better place.

▲ **HIDE-AND-SEEK** was a favorite game of John Jr. One of his favorite places to hide was under his dad's desk in the Oval Office, where the President worked.

CHAPTER FIVE

Life at the White HOUSE

The Kennedys brought a new spirit and excitement to the capital. Americans were excited to see a young family in the White House. The Kennedys had two children. Their daughter, Caroline, was just three years old when her father became President. Their son, John Jr., was only two months old. They were the first young children to live in the White House since the early 1900s.

Jackie added a preschool and kindergarten to the third floor

CAROLINE gives baby John a kiss after they moved to the White House. ▲

21

▲ **IMPORTANT VISITORS**
The President claps as John Jr. and Caroline skip around the Oval Office.

of the White House. There was also a new swimming
pool and a giant tree house. Even though he had a busy
schedule, President Kennedy always took time out of
his day to play with his children. Caroline rode her pet
pony, Macaroni, on the White House lawn. John Jr.
loved to play under the President's desk. Once he hid

there during a meeting his father was having with an important British leader. As the talks grew tense, little John jumped out from under the desk and screamed, "I'm a big bear and I'm hungry!" The President and his guest laughed. Kennedy told his visitor, "You may think this is strange behavior in the office of the President of the United States, but in addition to being the President, I also happen to be a father."

A Famous First Lady

The President and First Lady hosted many beautiful parties at the White House. They enjoyed music and invited different artists to perform at official dinners. Jackie Kennedy had a big influence on fashion. Women copied her style, from her clothes to the way she wore her hair.

People around the world were equally charmed

▲ COMMAND PERFORMANCE
The Kennedys entertained world leaders at the White House. After dinner they would often have a musician play. Here they are speaking with Pablo Casals, a famous cellist.

with the First Family. When the President visited world leaders, people were awestruck by the beautiful First Lady and the handsome and funny President. Thousands of French people poured into the streets to get a look at the couple during their trip to Paris in 1961. Jackie's every move was followed as if she were a movie star. At a news conference in Paris, the

President started a speech by saying jokingly, "I am the man who accompanied Jacqueline Kennedy to Paris."

President Kennedy and his family quickly became the closest thing the United States had to royalty. The White House was called Camelot during those years. It meant a time of fairy-tale splendor, hope, and great happiness.

▲ PARTY!
The Kennedys get ready for a state dinner. The man behind Jackie is Vice President Lyndon Johnson.

THE WHITE HOUSE TOUR

Jackie Kennedy was proud of the White House and wanted the inside to be as beautiful as the outside. She convinced people to donate the best American furniture, antiques, and artworks to the President's home.

In 1962 Jackie showed off the redecorated White House on television. For the first time, Americans could visit the President's home without leaving their living rooms. About eighty million people tuned in to watch this special broadcast.

Trouble Around the
WORLD

Ffrom the moment he became President, Kennedy was very focused on international problems. The United States and the Soviet Union were bitter rivals. The Soviet Union had a communist form of government, and the U.S. was a democracy. (In a communist country, people cannot vote for their leaders or own property like they can in a democracy.) The rivalry between the Soviet Union and the U.S. was called

◄ **FIDEL CASTRO** first came to power in Cuba in 1959. To get away from his rule, many Cubans came to the United States to live.

Dr. FIDEL CASTRO

▶ **ROBERT KENNEDY**
was the Attorney General,
the nation's top lawyer. He
also advised the President on
many issues. The two
brothers were very close.

the Cold War. No battles were actually fought between the two powers, but both countries tried to have more influence over the world. This led to serious military problems.

In 1961 Kennedy sent American troops to Cuba, a nation ninety miles off the coast of Florida. He wanted to overthrow Fidel Castro, the country's communist leader. Castro was supported by the Soviet Union. In the Bay of Pigs invasion, the U.S. helped a large group of Cubans try to get rid of Castro. But that did not happen. The President was upset. This was a big failure for him.

Cuba's Missiles

Less than a year later, the United States learned that the Soviet Union had sent dangerous nuclear weapons to Cuba. Some of the weapons were aimed at the United States. For days the world thought the United States and the Soviet Union might go to war. But Kennedy ended the crisis through talks with Soviet leader Nikita Khrushchev.

Another troubled place was Berlin. In 1947 this East German city had been split in two: communist-controlled East Berlin and free, democratic West Berlin. In 1961 the Soviets began to build a concrete wall

topped with sharp wire between the two sections of the city. They wanted to stop people from leaving East Berlin for West Berlin. The Berlin Wall became a symbol of

▲ EAST MET WEST when Kennedy met with the head of the Soviet Union, Nikita Khrushchev. They talked about the problems between their nations.

the struggle between communism and democracy. In June 1963 Kennedy went to Berlin. He promised that democracy would win out and the two sides of the city would be united someday. And he was right. Twenty-six years later, the wall was torn down. East and West Berlin were joined together again.

▼ A COUNTRY DIVIDED
President Kennedy visited Berlin, Germany, in 1963. He visited the Berlin Wall, which divided the city in two.

The Country Moves
AHEAD

There were problems around the world and problems at home as well. A young African American leader named Martin Luther King Jr. was leading a peaceful and fast-growing civil rights movement in the South. Blacks were tired of being treated like second-class citizens. They wanted to be

LINCOLN'S

▲ ABRAHAM LINCOLN was one of Kennedy's heroes.

On January 1, 1863, President Abraham Lincoln issued an Emancipation Proclamation. This statement set slaves in the South free. The proclamation did not totally end slavery in America, but it was a big step toward giving blacks basic freedoms. Many people criticized Lincoln because he freed only slaves who lived in

▲ KENNEDY fought for equal rights for African Americans. He often met with civil rights leaders about making peaceful changes. Martin Luther King Jr. is third from the left.

equal with white people. Segregation (keeping blacks and whites apart) was against the law in the United States. But it still took place in many southern states.

EMANCIPATION PROCLAMATION

southern states. But it did lead to the Thirteenth Amendment to the Constitution, which outlawed slavery in the United States in 1865. Despite winning freedom, blacks still had a long road ahead toward equality and civil rights.

▲ MARCH ON WASHINGTON
In August 1963, more than 250,000 people marched for civil rights.

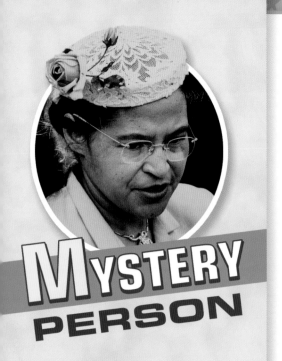

MYSTERY PERSON

CLUE 1: I am often called the "Mother of the Civil Rights Movement."

CLUE 2: On my way home from work on December 1, 1955, I was arrested in Montgomery, Alabama, for refusing to give up my bus seat to a white passenger.

CLUE 3: My arrest led blacks to stop using the bus system. They demanded that buses no longer be separated into different sections for whites and blacks. The bus boycott started the push for equal rights for blacks all over the South.

Who am I?

ANSWER: ROSA PARKS

In some places African Americans were refused jobs because of their skin color. They were not allowed to go to the same schools or restaurants as white people. They had to sit in the back of the bus or give up their seats to white people. African Americans couldn't drink from the same water fountain or use the same bathroom as whites. They couldn't stay in the same hotels. They had to use separate waiting rooms in bus stations. Some people made it hard for blacks to vote in elections.

Protesters decided to do something about these problems. In many southern cities, African Americans refused to ride city buses. They began

protests and strikes to tell the world about the unfairness. This was often met by anger on the part of some white people. Many African Americans were yelled at or beaten for trying to get equal rights.

Kennedy was very angry that black people had fewer opportunities, based on the color of their skin. He decided strong U.S. government action needed to be taken. "One hundred years of delay have passed since President Lincoln freed the slaves, yet their heirs, their grandsons are not fully free," he said. In 1963 President Kennedy proposed a civil rights bill that was later passed by the United States Congress.

The bill called for strong laws to protect the rights of African Americans and to make sure blacks and whites could go to the same schools.

The Race for Space

After sending the first human into orbit, the Soviet Union was ahead of the United States in exploring space. President Kennedy wanted the U.S. to lead in space exploration. In 1961 he asked Congress for money to help build rockets.

He said, "I believe this nation should commit itself to achieving the goal, before this decade is out, of landing a man on the moon and returning him safely to the Earth."

Just a few years earlier, Kennedy's bold idea might have seemed impossible. But within one year of his speech to Congress, John Glenn became the first American to orbit the Earth. And in 1969 two American astronauts became the first people to walk on the moon—and return safely to Earth.

Kennedy's dream had come true. Space was finally being explored!

◀ THE APOLLO 11 CREW pose proudly in their spacesuits. Michael Collins (center) piloted the spacecraft, while Neil Armstrong (left) and Edwin "Buzz" Aldrin (right) walked on the moon.

JOHN F. KENNEDY ★ ★ CHAPTER EIGHT

A Tragic
TRIP

November 22, 1963, was a clear, sunny day in Dallas, Texas. President Kennedy and the First Lady traveled to the city on a speaking tour. Many people in Texas did not agree with the President's policies on civil rights and other issues. Kennedy hoped to gain support by traveling there.

Tens of thousands of people came out to greet the President. They cheered, clapped, and carried welcome signs. Kennedy sat in the back

▲ ARRIVAL IN DALLAS
The Kennedys leave Air Force One—the President's personal plane.

of a black convertible with Jackie and waved to the crowds. Suddenly gunshots pierced through the cheering crowds. President Kennedy had been shot twice! He was rushed to a hospital, but doctors could not save him. John Fitzgerald Kennedy died at the age of forty-six.

◄ **VICE PRESIDENT LYNDON JOHNSON** is sworn in as President on board Air Force One. His wife, Lady Bird, is on the left. Mrs. Kennedy is on the right.

The President's suspected killer, Lee Harvey Oswald, was caught and arrested immediately. Oswald was later shot and killed by another man. (To this day some people believe that Oswald did not act alone in the shooting. But that has never been proven.)

Vice President Lyndon Johnson, his wife, and Jackie Kennedy were taken back to Air Force One. On board the

▲ JOHN KENNEDY JR. salutes his father's coffin at the funeral. This famous photograph touched the hearts of many Americans.

JOHN, JACKIE, & CAROLINE

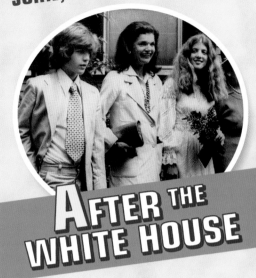

AFTER THE WHITE HOUSE

◄ PRESIDENT KENNEDY'S body was placed in a coffin covered with an American flag. After being taken from the White House, the coffin traveled along the funeral route by horse-drawn carriage as people tearfully watched.

plane, Johnson was sworn in as the thirty-sixth President of the United States.

The entire world mourned the loss of the beloved young President Kennedy. In shock and grief, leaders from many nations came to the funeral.

Hundreds of thousands of people lined the streets of Washington, D.C., to pay their respects as the President's coffin slowly wound its way through the capital. Millions more watched on television as the nation came to a full

Eleven days after the President's death, Jackie, Caroline, and John Jr. moved out of the White House. Jackie wanted her kids to succeed in whatever they decided to do. "Just remember how proud your father was and would have been, and never forget that," she told them. Jackie went on to have a successful career as a book editor. She died in 1994 at the age of sixty-five. John Jr. went to law school and started a magazine. He died in a plane crash in 1999. Caroline is married with three children. She is a lawyer and author who works hard to keep alive the special memories of her family.

▲ JOHN KENNEDY was often happiest and most relaxed when he was sailing. He loved the sea.

stop in memory of the President. A riderless black horse slowly walked behind the coffin. It was a symbol of a fallen leader.

The First Lady walked behind the coffin for more

► **THE PRESIDENT** was remembered on this cover of LIFE magazine, on U.S. half dollars, and on postage stamps.

LIFE

PRESIDENT
JOHN F.
KENNEDY
—
1917
1963

NOVEMBER 29 · 1963 · 25¢

than a mile. Jackie stayed strong through the terrible tragedy. Her strength and grace during that terrible time brought comfort to the entire country.

Kennedy Remembered

John Fitzgerald Kennedy was President of the United States for just over one thousand days. During that time, he made a strong impression on the nation and the world. President Kennedy will always be remembered for his ability to get people to do their

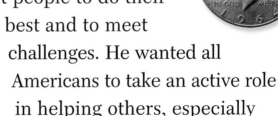

best and to meet challenges. He wanted all Americans to take an active role in helping others, especially those who are less fortunate.

Shortly before his death Kennedy said, "A man may die, nations may rise and fall, but an idea lives on."

Talking About
KENNEDY

▲ Hugh Sidey

TIME For Kids editor Dina El Nabli and Kid Reporter Daniel Bonner spoke with Hugh Sidey, a reporter who knew John F. Kennedy and wrote a book about his presidency. Here's what Sidey had to say.

Q: *What is your fondest memory of President Kennedy?*
A: Once I went to interview him, and he said, "Let's take a swim." That's the only underwater interview I've ever had.

Q: *What did the Kennedys bring to the White House that was unique?*
A: The Kennedys realized that part of the American dream was the search for beauty in everyday doings.

▶ THE SPACE SHUTTLE *ATLANTIS* takes off. Many people say it's because of John F. Kennedy that we have explored space.

Q: *What do you think JFK would be fighting for today?*

A: To save the environment, limit nuclear arms, and make sure that everybody has equal opportunities.

Q: *Is there a program, like the Peace Corps, that President Kennedy would support today?*

A: Kennedy might have been very interested in a national service program of some kind. Every young person would have to sign up as a volunteer and serve in some way at home or abroad. He believed people should do good for others.

◀ AMERICANS join the Peace Corps in order to help others. The Corps, started by Kennedy, is still going strong.

43

JOHN F. KENNEDY'S
KEY DATES

1917 Born on May 29, in Brookline, Massachusetts

1940 Graduates from Harvard; publishes *Why England Slept*

1943 Leads navy ship crew to safety

1946 Elected to United States Congress

1952 Elected to United States Senate

1953 Marries Jacqueline Bouvier

1957 Wins Pulitzer Prize for *Profiles in Courage*

1961 Inaugurated as President

1962 Cuban missile crisis

1963 Proposes civil rights bill; assassinated on November 22, in Dallas, Texas

1920 Women get the right to vote in the United States.

1950 Korean War begins.

1955 Elvis Presley becomes the first rock star.